Leabharlainn nan Eilean Siar

WITHDRAWN

TDF

J 30877188
SCHOOL
LIBRARY
STOCK

D1421428

Nature's Cycles

The Rock Cycle

Sally Morgan

WAYLAND

WESTERN ISLES LIBRARIES	
30877188J	
Bertrams	03.09.08
J552	£12.99

WITHDRAWN

First published in 2008
by Wayland

Copyright © Wayland 2008

Wayland
338 Euston Road
London NW1 3BH

Wayland Australia
Level 17/207 Kent Street
Sydney, NSW 2000

All rights reserved

Series editor: Nicola Edwards
Designer: Jason Billin

Picture acknowledgements: Cover: Main image
Genevieve Leaper/Ecoscene; stones Anthony
Cooper/Ecoscene; tor Andrew Brown/Ecoscene; lava
Robert Nichol/ Ecoscene

Title page Genevieve Leaper/Ecoscene; p4 Andrew
Brown/ Ecoscene; p5, p6 Andrew Brown/ Ecoscene; p7t
John Farmar/ Ecoscene, p7b. Anthony Cooper/
Ecoscene; p8t Erik Schaffer/ Ecoscene, p8b Kevin
King/ Ecoscene; p9 top clock Chinch Gryniewicz/
Ecoscene, Angela Hampton/ Ecoscene,.Sally Morgan/
Ecoscene, Chinch Gryniewicz/ Ecoscene; p11t Andrew
Brown/ Ecoscene; p11b Erik Schaffer/ Ecoscene; p12
Robert Nichol/ Ecoscene - also on contents; p13t
Wayne Lawler/ Ecoscene; p13b Quentin Bates/
Ecoscene; p14 Ecoscene - Papilio /Robert Pickett; p15
Nick Hawkes/ Ecoscene; p16 Genevieve Leaper/
Ecoscene; p17 Paul Thompson/ Ecoscene; p18t Sally
Morgan/ Ecoscene; p18b. Martin Jones/ Ecoscene; p19
Fritz Polking/ Ecoscene; p20 Andrew Brown/ Ecoscene;
p21t Fritz Polking/ Ecoscene; p21b. Peter McGrath/
Ecoscene; p22, p23 (both) John Farmar/ Ecoscene;
p24 Chris Chelmick/ Ecoscene; p25, p26 Peter Hulme/
Ecoscene; p27t Sally Morgan/ Ecoscene; p27, p28
Nick Hawkes/ Ecoscene; p29 Judyth Platt/ Ecoscene

Artwork by Ian Thompson

British Library Cataloguing in Publication Data

Morgan, Sally
The rock cycle. - (Nature's cycles)
1. Rock life cycles - Juvenile literature
I. Title
571.8'2

ISBN: 978 0 7502 5359 8

Printed in China

Wayland is a division of Hachette Children's Books,
an Hachette Livre UK company.

Contents

What is a rock?

Rocks are everywhere, in the ground beneath our feet and in gardens and parks. They form mountains and cliffs. Some are used to build structures and others are so attractive that they are made into jewellery.

Inside a rock

A rock is made of minerals. Minerals are natural substances that occur in the ground. They are neither animal nor plant but substances such as salt, metal or sulphur. Coal is a mineral made of carbon, while the mineral quartz contains almost pure silica. Rocks differ in the minerals that they contain and each rock has its own distinctive mix of minerals.

Rocks usually occur as large masses. Natural processes break rocks down into smaller fragments, which we call stones and pebbles. Even smaller fragments of rock form sand, silt and clay.

⬤ Water is an important part of the rock cycle as running water wears away rocks.

In Focus: Rock as a habitat

Rocks provide important habitats for plants and animals. There are lots of cracks running through a mass of rock. Water and soil collect in these cracks. Large cracks on the surface of a rock are perfect places for small plants such as mosses and ferns to grow. However there is too little soil for larger plants. Animals such as woodlice and spiders are found in the cracks too, sheltering from the sun and wind. Birds nest on ledges on a rock face.

🔺 Many mountain ranges are formed from granite rock such as this one in the French Alps.

Ancient rocks

Most rocks are millions of years old. Many were formed before the dinosaurs existed. We know this because scientists have found embedded in rocks the fossil remains of strange animals that lived in the oceans hundreds of millions of years ago.

Investigate: Carbon

Carbon is a very common element that is found in the ground. It occurs in several forms such as diamonds, graphite, coal and charcoal. Use the Internet to find out more about the different forms of carbon and the uses to which they can be put.

The rock cycle

The rock cycle begins with the formation of the rocks. Some are formed quickly in just a few weeks but others are formed very slowly, over millions of years. Many rocks are hidden beneath the Earth's surface. The rocks that lie on the surface are exposed to wind and water, and they get worn away, or eroded. Fragments of rock such as pebbles and sand are carried away and end up in rivers and then the sea. There, these particles of rocks eventually form new rocks.

Rocks beneath our feet

Rock is found underneath every surface. If you dig a hole in the ground, you eventually come to a layer of hard rock beneath the soil. In most places the rock is covered by soil. However, where the rock is not covered it forms features such as cliffs and mountain tops.

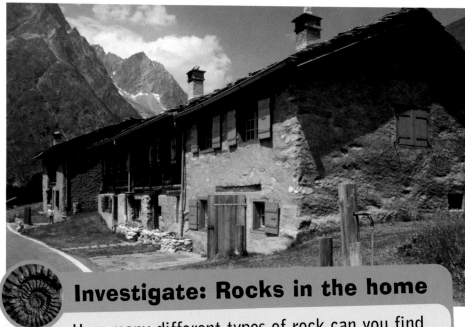
▼ This traditional alpine house in Switzerland is made from local stone.

Rocks for building

Most rocks are hard and have many uses. They are ideal building materials as they are hard-wearing and most are impermeable. This means that water runs off them rather than through them. Rocks can be used to make walls of buildings to keep out the rain, wind and sun. They are used as a flooring material too. For example, sandstone is cut into thin layers called flagstones and laid over the floor. In many hot countries such as Morocco and Spain, homes have smooth marble floors that are cool in summer.

Investigate: Rocks in the home

How many different types of rock can you find in your home? Have a look at the walls, are they made from stone or brick? Remember that concrete contains sand and gravel. There may be decorative items made of rocks, such as granite and marble or jewellery with precious stones. Feel each rock that you find. Is it smooth, rough, hard or soft?

Sand and gravel

Sand and gravel are two essential materials used by the building industry. The only difference between sand and gravel is the size of the rock particles. Sand is made up of small grains of rock, while gravel is formed from larger particles such as pebbles. Sand and gravel have many uses, such as making paths and children's sand pits, and they are essential for making concrete. Concrete is an important building material. To make concrete, sand and gravel are mixed with cement and water. The runny mix hardens to form a solid stone-like material.

In Focus: Precious gemstones

Diamonds, emeralds and rubies are just three examples of precious stones. The minerals that make up precious gemstones give colour and catch the light. This makes the stones are attractive and valuable. Often the gemstone that is dug straight from the ground looks nothing like the stone that is used in jewellery. The raw stones have to be cleaned, cut and polished to produce the final stone.

⬣ A quarry is a place where rock is dug out of the ground.

⬤ Diamonds, opals and emeralds have been used in these pieces of jewellery.

7

Rock types

There are many different types of rock and they are grouped according to how they were formed and the mix of minerals that they contain.

Minerals

There are more than 3,000 different minerals in existence, but only about 30 are found in rocks. Some rocks contain several minerals, but other rocks are made from just one or two different minerals. If you looked closely at a piece of granite rock with a magnifying glass you would see that it is made up of several different minerals including mica, quartz and feldspar. Each mineral is of a slightly different colour and size, and they are all stuck together.

Rock properties

Rocks vary in their hardness and ability to take up water. A piece of chalk for example, is quite soft and you can scrape the surface with a fingernail. In contrast, diamond is one of the hardest substances, so hard that it is used in industry to cut through metal and stone. Diamond powder is used as an abrasive to produce a smooth surface. Rocks such as basalt are incredibly heavy, while pumice is full of air so it is incredibly light. Some rocks are porous. This means that the spaces between the minerals can become filled with water. Chalk is a porous rock.

Permeable rocks allow water to flow through them. Chalk, limestone and sandstone are permeable rocks. This limits their usefulness. For example, limestone and chalk are not used as worktops in kitchens as they take up liquids and stain easily. Most rocks, such as slate, are impermeable. Slate is used to make roofing tiles because it keeps water out.

◭ Quartz is formed of silicon dioxide and is the most common mineral on Earth.

◮ This home is close to a crumbling cliff and soon it will fall into the sea.

Forming rocks

Although there are many types of rock, they are formed in just one of three ways. Igneous rocks are formed when molten (liquid) magma from deep in the Earth cools and becomes solid. Sedimentary rocks form over millions of years from layers of sediment. Metamorphic rocks are igneous or sedimentary rocks that have been altered in some way by natural processes. The following pages will explore how the different types of rocks are formed and how they differ from each other.

Investigate: Rock features

Collect some samples of different rocks such as chalk, slate, granite and marble. First test how hard each is by scratching the surface with a sharp object. Can you see a mark on the rock surface? Now see if each is porous by carefully dripping one drop of water onto the surface of the rock. Does the water disappear? Can you think of a use for a porous rock?

The Rock Cycle

Rocks are broken into smaller pieces by water and ice.

Water wears away the rock and carries small particles to the sea.

Layers of sand build up on the sea floor and in time form rock. When the land is uplifted, the rock may appear above ground.

Igneous rocks

Deep inside the Earth it is so hot that the rock is liquid. Liquid rock is called magma. Magma is less dense than the rock lying above it, so it flows up through cracks towards the surface.

Crystals

As magma moves towards the surface, it cools. In some places, the magma explodes out of cracks as lava. In other places the magma is trapped in pockets in the ground. As the magma cools, crystals appear. The crystallisation process continues until all the magma is solid and has formed an igneous rock.

Igneous rocks vary in the size of their crystals. If the magma cools quickly, for example if magma pours into the cold water of an ocean, the crystals are small, while magma that cools slowly in the ground has larger crystals of more than 20 millimetres across.

🔺 Some magma is forced up to the surface and pours out of the ground as lava. Over time layers of lava build up and form a volcano. Some magma remains trapped underground where it cools and forms rock.

In Focus: Inside the Earth

The uppermost layer in the Earth is called the crust. It is up to 90 kilometres thick under the continents and about 6 km thick under the oceans. About 95 per cent of the Earth's crust is made up of igneous rock. Beneath the crust is the mantle, a layer which is 3000 km thick. The magma in the mantle is very thick and slow-moving, a bit like treacle.

Intrusive rocks

Igneous rocks that form deep in the ground are called intrusive igneous rocks. They are ancient rocks that have cooled and solidified over millions of years. Most intrusive igneous rocks remain hidden, often under a layer of sedimentary rock. However, movements in the Earth's crust can cause the igneous rocks to be thrust upwards. When the overlying rocks are worn away by wind and water the igneous rocks are exposed.

Granites, gabbros and kimberlites are examples of intrusive igneous rocks. The four main minerals in granite are feldspar, quartz, biotite and muscovite. Gabbro contains large crystals, more than 1 mm in size. This dark, often greenish rock is rich in minerals such as chromium, nickel, cobalt, gold, silver and platinum. Intrusive igneous rocks are often rich in precious gemstones such as diamonds, topaz and emerald. For example, diamonds are found in kimberlite.

⬤ The Cheesewring in Cornwall is a pile of granite rocks known as a tor. All the surrounding softer rock has been eroded leaving just the granite.

⬤ If you look at a piece of granite through a magnifying glass you will see it is made up of many different minerals.

Investigate: Granite

Granite is used in kitchens and bathrooms as a decorative and hard-wearing rock for work surfaces. There are up to 100 different types of granite, each differing in its mineral content. The colours range from virtually pink to jet black. Use the Internet to search for websites that sell granite. Look at the photographs of the different colours of granite that are available. See if you can find out how the minerals in a black granite differ from those in a pink granite.

Volcanic rocks

Volcanic eruptions are impressive but frightening natural events. The lava that escapes from a volcano is magma that has reached the surface. The lava may explode from the volcano or flow out of cracks. Rivers of lava run down the sides of the volcano.

From lava to rock

When the lava cools it forms extrusive igneous rock or volcanic rock. Usually the lava cools slowly over weeks or even months. Sometimes the lava cools in just a few days and there is no time for the minerals in the lava to form crystals. When this happens the lava forms a type of volcanic glass called obsidian.

Obsidian is a very dense rock which does not allow light to pass through it. This means it looks almost black. However a tiny sliver of obsidian is transparent because the light can pass straight through.

◀ Red hot lava flows from a Hawaiian volcano into the sea.

The fertile soils around this volcano in Indonesia are used to grow rice.

In Focus: Volcanoes and lava

The lava that forms volcanoes is weathered by the wind and rain. The lava breaks up and soil starts to form. In time, the slopes of volcanoes such as Mount Teide in Tenerife and Mount Etna in Sicily become covered in soils that are used to grow crops and vines. However, these two volcanoes are still active and are likely to produce new lava that would be a threat to the people living close by.

When lava cools slowly, small crystals form. The most common volcanic rock is basalt which has crystals so small that they cannot be seen with the eye alone. Basalt forms from dark, thick lava that is rich in iron and magnesium. The black sand on some Hawaiian beaches comes from weathered basalt. Pumice is another volcanic rock which has tiny crystals. It is a pale rock that is very light in weight because it is full of tiny holes. The holes were left when the volcanic gases bubbled out.

Investigate: Pumice

Pumice has many uses in cosmetics. Pumice stones can be bought as exfoliants to rub dry skin off the soles of feet. It is also used in toothpaste and hand cleaners. You can buy pumice stones from chemist shops. Look closely to see the tiny holes in the pumice. Will the stone float in water? Soak your feet in water and then see if you can remove rough skin with the pumice.

The hexagonal columns forming this cliff in Iceland are made from basalt.

Sedimentary rocks

Sedimentary rocks cover about three-quarters of the world's surface. The most common sedimentary rock is shale. This rock makes up half of all sedimentary rocks. About 30 per cent of sedimentary rocks are sandstones and 20 per cent are limestones. Sedimentary rocks are made up of many tiny particles of rock that are stuck together.

▼ If you break open a piece of limestone you may be lucky enough to find a fossil.

Layers of rock

Sedimentary rocks form under large bodies of water over millions of years. The first stage in the formation of a sedimentary rock is the building up of a layer of sediment on the bottom of lakes and seas. The sediment contains sand, silt and clay, which have come from rocks. The remains of dead plants and animals drop to the sea or lake bed too, and add to the sediment.

In Focus: Fossils

When marine animals become fossilised, the soft parts of their bodies break down, but the hard parts, such as the shells, remain. A fossil is an exact copy of the original animal except that it is hard and rock-like. Common fossils in limestone are ammonites and trilobites, animals that were common in the oceans 300 million years ago.

From sediment to rock

As more sediment collects, the lower layers are squashed by
the weight of all the overlying layers. In time, thick layers of
sediment build up. The sediments become rocks when all the
particles are stuck together. The 'glue' comes from the various
minerals in the sediment. For example, sandstone contains
grains of quartz that are glued together with silica and calcite.

Investigate: Layered rocks

In this investigation you will make sedimentary rock. Take a
1.5l plastic bottle, sand, four different food colourings and some wall
filler. Wear a pair of plastic gloves to mix one of the food colours into
some sand and filler and pour it into the bottom of the plastic bottle.
Add more layers, each time using a different colour, until you reach
the top of the bottle. Leave to harden for a few days, then cut away
the plastic bottle to reveal the layers of sedimentary rocks.

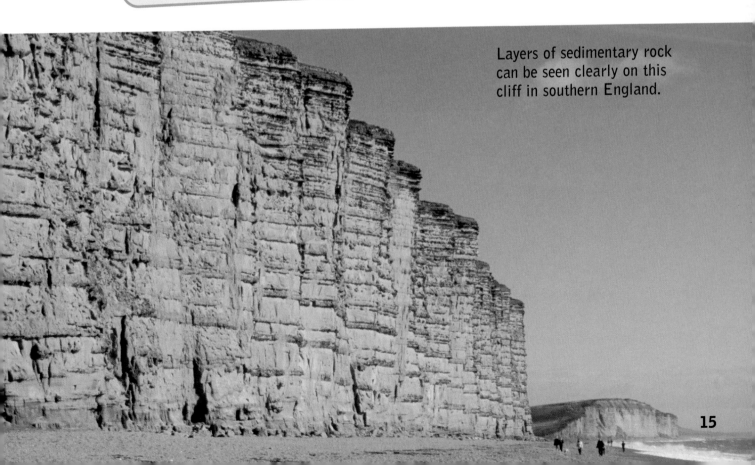

Layers of sedimentary rock
can be seen clearly on this
cliff in southern England.

Changing rocks

Rocks can be changed by forces such as the heat from a volcano or from the pressures exerted when two sections of the Earth's crust push against each other. The rocks are altered so much that they turn into a new type of rock. These rocks are metamorphic, or changed, rocks.

Moving plates

The Earth's crust is a thin layer that floats on the magma in the mantle. The crust is broken into large pieces called plates. As the magma moves around, it causes the plates to move too. When two plates collide with each other the crust is pushed up and mountains are formed. For example, the Himalayas have been formed by the Indian plate moving north and pushing against the Asian plate, causing the crust in between to crumple and push up to form a mountain range. This has happened very slowly, over millions of years. The process is still continuing as the Himalayas are becoming taller by a few centimetres every year.

○ The highest mountain peak in the world is Everest in the Himalayas. Mount Everest, which is to the left of the centre of this photograph, is 8848 m (29,028 ft) high.

The effects of change

When rocks are changed by pressure or heat, they often become tougher and more crystalline. For example, heat changes sandstone to a hard metaquartzite, while intense pressure changes limestone into marble. Rocks that are changed by pressure are crushed and they take on a banded or layered appearance. Pressure changes mudstone and shale into slate. If there is even more pressure, mudstone becomes a type of rock called gneiss. It has a banded appearance with layers of different minerals. The pressure can cause fossils in the rock to be distorted or twisted.

In Focus: Earthquakes

Earthquakes are caused by the Earth's plates moving past each other. During an earthquake the ground shakes, buildings collapse and large cracks appear in the ground. Most of the world's earthquakes occur around the edge of the Pacific plate, affecting South East Asia, Australia, Japan, Canada, the USA and South America. The fourth most powerful earthquake since 1900 occurred under the Indian Ocean in 2004. It caused the tsunami that killed more than 200,000 people in Indonesia, Thailand and Sri Lanka. In 2005, powerful earthquakes rocked the Himalayas and the island of Sumatra in Indonesia.

Investigate: Marble

Marble is a very popular building material as it is hard and can be polished to give a smooth, shiny surface. Its name comes from the Greek word meaning 'shining stone'. Many places or structures have marble in their name, for example Marble Arch in London. Can you find some examples of places or structures that have marble in their name and some pictures of buildings that are built from marble?

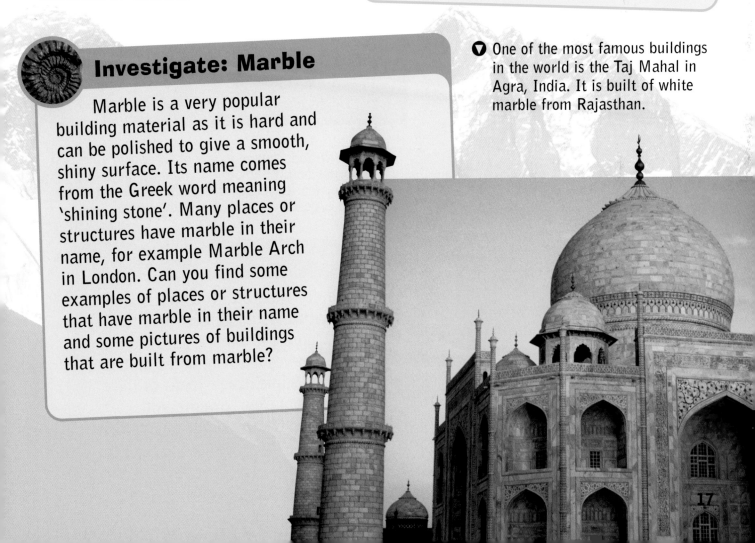

⊘ One of the most famous buildings in the world is the Taj Mahal in Agra, India. It is built of white marble from Rajasthan.

Worn away

The next stage in the rock cycle occurs when rocks are exposed to sun, wind and rain and they are worn away. This is called weathering or erosion. Some rocks are weathered more readily, for example chalk, while others such as granite are tough and resistant to weather.

Flowing water

Water running over a rock slowly wears it away. This is because the water carries particles, such as grains of sand, that rub the surface. The rocks at the bottom of a stream have been worn smooth by flowing water. Over millions of years, the power of fast-flowing water along a river erodes any rock along the sides and the bottom, creating banks and even deep gorges.

◯ The Grand Canyon is one of the world's deepest gorges and it has been formed by the River Colorado. Layers of different sedimentary rock are exposed on the sides of the gorge.

Investigate: Weathering

Different types of rock weather at different rates. Rain water is very slightly acidic and the acids in water react with the calcium carbonate in limestone, leaving a rough, pitted surface. Granites are more hard-wearing. Have a look at the different gravestones in a graveyard. The dates on the gravestones will tell you how old they are. Find some gravestones of the same age but made from different rock, such as marble, granite and limestone. Which ones are more weathered? Look for discolouring, pitted surfaces and crumbling edges.

Shattering rocks

Water can break up huge blocks of rock too. Water seeps through cracks in rock. When temperatures fall to freezing, any water in the cracks turns to ice. When water freezes it expands, so the ice pushes on the surrounding rock and opens up the crack. When the ice melts, the rock shatters. This process is called freeze-thaw.

Mountain slopes are often covered by rock fields made up of lots of small broken rocks. These rock fields are created by freeze-thaw in the rock cliffs. The bits of rock break off and tumble down onto the slope below. These slopes are very unstable and only the most nimble of animals, such as mountain goats, can cross them.

Wind action

Wind can erode rocks too. This is because wind picks up tiny particles from the ground and rubs them against rocks. Over time the rocks are worn away. Desert rocks often have a shiny surface called desert varnish that is created by the erosion. Also, wind erosion can create grooves and depressions in the rock which get larger over time, creating interesting rock shapes.

⭕ The action of water over thousands of years has eroded the rock in this part of Utah, USA, leaving white limestone spires that look like giant toadstools.

In Focus: Sand blasting

Stone that has become dirty with grime can be cleaned using a method called sand blasting. This mimics the natural process of wind erosion by directing a jet of sand at the surface of the stone. The particles of sand wear away the dirty top layer, revealing a clean surface underneath.

Weathered shapes

The weathering of rocks by wind and water has created some of the world's best known landscapes. The National Parks of central North America are home to amazing natural arches, canyons and weird rock shapes that attract millions of visitors each year. Weathering takes place underground too, creating caves.

Rock arches

Arches National Park in the USA has more than 2,000 sandstone arches. Over millions of years, water has seeped through the soft sandstone rocks, opening up cracks and causing huge boulders to drop away. Wind has blown away all the fine particles and this has smoothed the surface of the rock. Over time, this has created the arches. There are single and double arches, windows and columns. The erosion is still continuing and since 1970 almost 50 arches have collapsed.

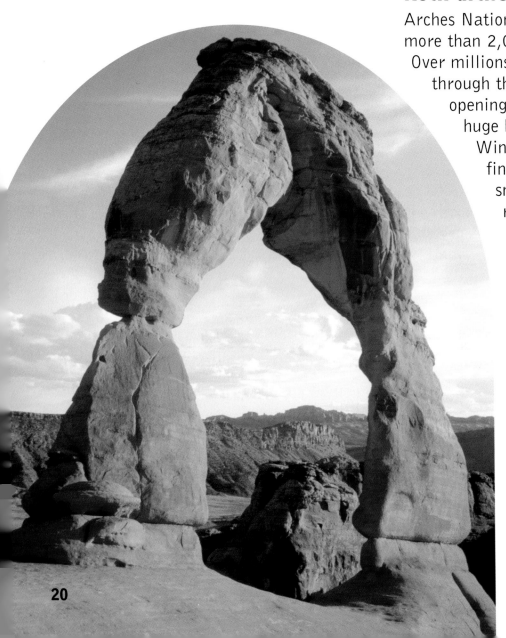

◀ Delicate Arch is the most famous arch in Arches National Park. There was an idea to protect the arch by coating it in plastic to protect it from erosion. However, the suggestion was thought to be impractical and was not put into practice.

In Focus: Rock landscapes and tourism

Millions of people visit the rock landscapes of the Grand Canyon, Arches National Park and Bryce Canyon in the United States. However there has to be a balance between conserving the landscape and allowing people to enjoy it. As people walk over the rocks their feet erode the surface, just like water and wind. Climbing can dislodge rocks, damage arches and open up more cracks to water. In the National Parks, the areas over which people can roam are restricted to certain paths, so the landscape is protected.

⊙ This narrow canyon in Arizona, USA, has been carved by wind and rain, leaving behind a wonderful corkscrew-like surface to the sandstone rock.

Forming caves

Most caves form in soft rock such as limestone. Water seeping down through cracks dissolves the surface of the limestone, making the cracks larger. When the crack is large enough water can flow through the rock. The cracks become larger still and an underground stream forms. As more rock is worn away a network of caves, underground passages and streams is formed.

Investigate: Conserving buildings

Next time you visit an ancient monument or historic building, look at the features that are made from stone, such as steps, floors and walls. Notice how the rubbing of feet over hundreds of years has made stone steps and floors shiny. Are there signs of the stone being worn away? Look at the edges of stone walls near entrances. The action of hundreds of people rubbing past gradually wears away the stone. Look for ways in which the structure of the building is protected, for example by the placing clear sheets of Perspex over stone walls so they are protected but can still be seen.

Washed up

The particles that are created by weathering have an important role to play in the rock cycle. They are blown away by the wind or carried by water and end up in rivers and the sea. The particles build up layers of sediment that in time turn into sedimentary rock.

Meandering rivers

A fast-flowing stream tumbling down a mountainside picks up particles which are carried downstream. Some rivers carry so many particles that their waters are murky. For example, the Huang Ho River in China is also called the Yellow River because it carries so much silt.

As a river gets nearer to the sea, the water flows more slowly. It may meander, or form snake-like loops, across the land. When water flows around a bend in the river, the flow is fastest on the outside of the bend and slowest on the inside. Sediment is dropped on the inside bend and this builds up to form sand banks. Even more sediment is dropped when the river reaches the sea. The sediment builds up to form a muddy estuary.

⊙ This river is meandering across a valley as it nears the sea.

In Focus: The importance of mud

When a river reaches the sea, the sediment is dropped. Over time the sediment builds up into banks of sticky mud called mud flats. At low tide, the mud flats are exposed. Mud is important for wildlife as it is full of nutrients. Marine animals such as lugworms and cockles live in the mud. In turn they are fed upon by wading birds such as dunlin, shelduck and knot. There are seals and turtles and plenty of fish too. Flatfish such as plaice and sole hide under the surface of the sediment and catch small animals.

Changing coastlines

Rocks that form coastlines are under constant attack from the waves. Harder rocks erode more slowly and they form headlands which stick out from the coast while softer rocks are worn away and this creates an indentation on the coast called a bay.

All the eroded particles of rock are carried by the tides into the bays to form beaches. The sand on a beach is always moving. When waves hit a coastline at an angle, the sand is carried along the coast. In some places the sand builds up to form new beaches, but on other parts of the coast sand may be carried away.

⊙ Lulworth Cove in England was formed by the sea eroding the softer rock to form the bay, leaving the harder rock as headlands.

Investigate: Pebbly beaches

Pebbles on a beach are moved around by the waves and they are gradually sorted by their size. The larger pebbles are moved higher up the beach than the smaller ones. Next time you visit a pebbly beach, look closely at the pebbles. Start at the water's edge and measure the diameter of 10 pebbles. Measure another 10 pebbles on the middle of the beach and then 10 from the top of the beach. Work out the average diameter of the 10 pebbles (add up the 10 values and divide by 10). Does the size change from the top to the bottom?

⊙ The pebbles on this beach have been sorted according to their size by the water.

Soil

Weathering is an important part of the rock cycle. Many of the weathered particles of rock end up in water and form new sedimentary rocks. However weathering can also lead to the formation of soil.

Soil formation

When rocks are exposed to the weather, they crumble and become covered with a layer of rock fragments. Plants start to grow amongst the fragments. Dead leaves get mixed in too. Over thousands, even millions of years, the soil becomes thicker. The speed with which the soil forms depends on many factors. These include the type of rock, the climate, how much plant and animal activity is taking place, and whether the soil is on the level or on a slope.

In Focus: Soil organisms

As many as one billion bacteria may be found in just one gram of soil. There are larger animals too, such as thread-like nematode worms, ants, beetle larvae, and most importantly, earthworms. Earthworms burrow through the soil and are important for mixing the organic matter into the soil and creating air spaces and helping drainage. This improves the soil for plants.

◀ This alpine plant is growing between the rocks, trapping water and leaves. In time a thin soil builds up.

Some of the youngest soils are those that are forming on lava and on sand dunes. Among the oldest, that are thousands of years old, are the deep black soils of the Prairies in the United States.

Sand, silt and clay

Soil contains three types of particle: sand, silt and clay, of which clay is the smallest. There is organic matter too. This is the decayed remains of plants and animals. Soil particles are round in shape so there are plenty of air spaces and water around them too.

Soil erosion

Soil may take a long time to form, but it can be washed away in a matter of days. Most soils are covered by plants, which help to protect the soil from the sun, wind and rain. Plant roots hold the soil particles together. When the plants are removed, the soil is dried by the sun, then blown away by wind. Water washes soil away, especially on slopes.

Investigate: Soil

To see if a soil contains large amounts of sand or clay, try these simple tests. Take a handful of soil. Does it crumble easily in your hand? What is the texture of the soil? Make the soil wet and see if you can shape the soil with your fingers. Now place some soil in a small plastic plant pot with holes in the bottom and add some water. How quickly does the water drain away? A sandy soil is very crumbly, has a gritty texture and drains quickly. A clay soil feels smooth, it will not crumble, and it can be moulded into shapes with the fingers. Water drains slowly through a clay soil.

Dry sandy soil is easily blown away when it is left exposed without any plant cover.

Types of soil

There are many different soils around the world. They vary in depth and colour, and in the amount of sand, silt and clay that they contain.

Soil profiles

Soil is made up of distinct layers. On the top is a layer of dead and decaying matter such as leaf litter. Beneath this layer is the topsoil. The topsoil is dark in colour because it is rich in organic matter. Beneath the topsoil is the subsoil, which is much paler. The layer beneath the subsoil is very stony and below this is the bedrock.

Investigate: Soil profiles

Have a look at the profile of the soil in your garden or school grounds. Dig a deep hole with a spade. Make sure you cut vertically down one side of the hole so that you can see the layers clearly. Have a look at the profile. Can you see the topsoil and the subsoil?

◀ The top soil beneath the grass is a darker colour than the subsoil below.

— topsoil

— subsoil

Different soils

A podzol is an acid, sandy soil that forms under conifer forests and heathlands. A chernozem is a deep brown or black soil with a good mix of sand, silt and clay. It forms under grassland on the Prairies of North America and on the Steppes of Russia. Desert soils are very thin and lack organic matter. The heat draws water and salts into the topsoil. The water evaporates, leaving the salts behind on the surface.

Tropical soils

The intense heat and high rainfall in tropical areas causes rocks to be weathered more quickly than in other places. The rain washes away many of the useful minerals, such as potassium, and leaves behind iron and quartz. These minerals form a red soil called a laterite. Some laterites are very hard and can be cut into blocks and used as bricks. In part of Africa, hard laterite soils are used to form road surfaces.

⬥ Red laterite soils, seen here in Kenya, are clay soils with a high iron and aluminium content.

⬥ The dark brown, almost black colour of this soil is due to the presence of a lot of organic matter.

In Focus: Soils for farming

The best soils for farming are loams. A loam is a soil that has a good mix of sand, silt and clay. This means that the water drains through the soil, but not as quickly as in a sandy soil, nor does it get waterlogged like a clay soil. Farming soils have to be rich in organic matter and minerals so crop plants such as wheat and maize grow well. Some of the best farming soils are found in the Fens of Britain, on the North American Prairies and on the Russian Steppes.

Rocks and pollution

The rock cycle can be disrupted by air pollution. Air pollution harms plants and animals, and it damages rocks too. Exposed rock can be eroded by harmful substances in the air, such as sulphur dioxide. Sedimentary rocks such as limestone are the most vulnerable rocks.

City stones

The air in towns and cities is polluted by the exhausts of cars and emissions from power stations and other industries. Car exhausts pump out tiny particles of black soot and this makes the stone walls and statues dirty, giving them a black surface.

▷ The wall of this building in Oxford has been cleaned to reveal bright, clean stone.

In Focus: Repairing the damage

It is possible to repair some of the damage caused by air pollution. The grimy black coating that covers rocks can be blasted away using sand or water, to leave a new clean surface. However this cannot be done too many times, as each time a layer of rock is removed. When stones or statues have been badly damaged, the only way to repair the damage is to replace the stone, using rock of a similar origin.

Acid rain

Rain is naturally slightly acidic and it erodes rocks such as limestone (see pages 18-19). Acid rain is rain that is more acidic than normal. Pollutants such as sulphur dioxide and nitrous oxide rise into the atmosphere and dissolve in water to form weak acids. These acids fall to the ground in rain and wear away the surfaces of rock. Acid rain damages buildings in cities by dissolving the surface of stone, leaving it discoloured and pitted. Statues are worn smooth, so that the details on faces and hands are lost.

Around the world, historic buildings are under attack from air pollution. These include the Taj Mahal in India, mosques in North Africa, cathedrals and castles in United Kingdom, and marble monuments in Rome.

⬤ The features on this figurehead on Lincoln Castle can barely be seen as they have been damaged by air pollution.

Investigate: Lichens and air pollution

Lichens are organisms that are part plant and part fungus. There are many different types of lichen. There are encrusting lichens that are grey, yellow and orange in colour. Foliose lichens look like leaves. Others look like small balls of wool. Have a look at the buildings and trees where you live. The encrusting lichens can grow in polluted places, but the foliose lichens are very sensitive to air pollution. If you find any of the foliose lichens this means that the air is clean.

Glossary

abrasive A type of substance that is used to rub and grind another material to create a smooth surface.

acid rain Rain that is more acidic than normal due to the presence of weak acids.

bedrock The stony layer of soil beneath the subsoil.

cemented Stuck together, glued.

chernozem A deep dark brown-black soil that forms under grassland.

concrete A building material of sand, gravel, cement and water which is mixed together. It hardens and becomes stone-like.

crystallisation The process of forming crystals.

desert varnish The shiny surface on desert rocks which is created by erosion.

element A pure substance such as carbon that cannot be separated into any other substances.

erosion The wearing away of rock by wind and water.

estuary The place where a river empties into the sea.

exhaust Waste gases that are pumped out by the engines and chimneys of power stations and factories.

extrusive igneous rocks Rocks that form on the surface when lava cools and becomes solid.

fossil The remains of an animal or plant that are preserved in a rock.

freeze-thaw The action of freezing and then melting of water in rock.

gorge A narrow, steep-side valley with cliffs.

igneous rocks Rocks that are formed from magma. Granites and kimberlites are igneous rocks.

impermeable Not allowing water or other liquids to pass through. Slate is an impermeable rock.

intrusive igneous rocks Rocks that form in the ground when magma cools and becomes solid.

lava The molten (liquid) rocks that comes out of volcanoes. Magma is called lava when it reaches the surface.

lichens Organisms that are formed from an alga (a type of plant) and a fungus.

loam A soil that has a good mix of sand, silt and clay.

magma Molten or liquid rock beneath the Earth's surface.

meander To wind or bend.

metamorphic rocks Rocks that have undergone change, caused by intense heat or pressure. Marble is a metamorphic rock

mineral A natural, inorganic substance.

permeable Allowing water or other liquids to pass through. Limestone is a permeable rock

podzol An acidic soil that forms under heathland or conifer forests.

porous Having small pores or holes that allow water to seep through. Chalk is a porous rock.

quarry A large hole in the ground from which rocks are dug.

saturated Completely filled with water.

sediment Particles of sand, silt and clay that are carried by water and which settle on the bed of a lake, river or sea.

sedimentary rocks Rocks that are formed from layers of sediment. Shale is a sedimentary rock.

subsoil A lower layer of soil that has less organic matter than topsoil and lies above rock.

topsoil The uppermost layer of soil that is rich in organic matter.

tsunami A huge wave which is formed by an underwater earthquake.

volcano A crack in the Earth's crust through which lava escapes forming a mountain like structure. Shield volcanoes have a low shape while conical volcanoes are taller with steep sides.

weathering The wearing away or breaking down of rocks.

Further Information

Books

Soil, Geology Rocks! Rebecca Faulkner, Raintree 2007

Soil (Rocks and Minerals) Melissa Stewart, Heinemann Library 2003

Eyewitness: Rocks and Minerals, R.F. Symes, Dorling Kindersley 2004

Websites

The Learning Zone - Rocks
Oxford University Museum of Natural History
http://www.oum.ox.ac.uk/thezone/rocks/index.htm

Test your rock cycle knowledge.

Geology, Rocks, and Minerals
http://www.enchantedlearning.com/geology

Find out about rocks, minerals, soil and volcanoes.

The Rock Cycle
http://www.minsocam.org/MSA/K12/rkcycle/rkcycleindex.html

Information about the rock cycle presented by the Mineralogical Society of America.

Index